Celebrity Entrepreneurs

TAYLOR SWIFT

Tonya Maddox Cupp

Cavendish
Square

New York

Published in 2015 by Cavendish Square Publishing, LLC
243 5th Avenue, Suite 136, New York, NY 10016

Copyright © 2015 by Cavendish Square Publishing, LLC

First Edition

Library of Congress Cataloging-in-Publication Data

Cupp, Tonya Maddox.
Taylor Swift / Tonya Maddox Cupp.
pages cm. — (Celebrity entrepreneurs)
Includes index.
ISBN 978-1-50260-023-3 (hardcover) ISBN 978-1-50260-027-1 (paperback) ISBN 978-1-50260-028-8 (ebook)
1. Swift, Taylor, 1989—-Juvenile literature. 2. Country musicians—United States—Biography—Juvenile literature. I. Title.

ML3930.S989C87 2015
782.421642092—dc23
[B]

2014024958

Editor: Kristen Susienka
Copy Editor: Cynthia Roby
Art Director: Jeffrey Talbot
Designer: Joseph Macri
Senior Production Manager: Jennifer Ryder-Talbot
Production Editor: David McNamara
Photo Researcher: J8 Media

Printed in the United States of America

CONTENTS

Taylor sells out more shows than any other solo artist.

Taylor Swift: America's Sweetheart

For Taylor Swift, evolving from a shy Pennsylvania teenager into an internationally known singer and songwriter required careful thought, hard work, and determination. She practiced her guitar until her fingers bled. At age fourteen, driven by her dreams to write and record country music, she moved with her family to Nashville, Tennessee, where she agreed to make records for a brand new company. She became a songwriter, a singer, an actress, a shoe designer, a perfume creator, a philanthropist, and an **entrepreneur**.

For Taylor, being an entrepreneur means working hard even after awards have been won.

Country music legends Bill Anderson and Dolly Parton play the Grand Ole Opry.

It means taking chances. It also means defining a **brand** and staying true to it. Her fiery dedication to herself, her fans, and her image, as well as the way many of her fans have been able to form emotional connections with her songs, all help Taylor carve a special place in the **celebrity** scene. Through her music, business, **endorsements**, fashion, and more, Taylor Swift will likely remain in the public eye for years to come.

Country Music's Evolution

It's been hundreds of years since a man named Davy Crockett played his fiddle in Nashville.

A magnet for songwriters and musicians, the Music City has launched the careers of artists of many musical **genres** and sent them on worldwide tours. Nashville is also home to the Grand Ole Opry, the world's longest running live radio program, which has been running since 1925. It seems fitting that Taylor Swift would begin her music career in Nashville, too.

The music business has grown tremendously since the 1920s. Outdoor and recreation-hall concerts have evolved into international tours held in stadiums. Country music's popularity has waxed and waned over the years, but it is a form of art that has held its own.

Other forms of entertainment have also evolved over time, and Taylor has used her music success to become part of them as well. A movie is a movie, no matter what's onscreen, yet the business aspect of this form of entertainment has changed. The independent and documentary genres have become more popular over time, despite blockbusters and reboots. Taylor Swift's involvement in the film industry grew from her love of music and her popularity as "America's Sweetheart." This exposure has also led her to explore other industries, such as fashion and beauty.

Taylor's Influence on Music

On the radio, country has evolved to become America's most popular musical format, according to reports by *The New York Times*. As the general music industry continues to struggle financially, the country music audience has grown stronger, wider, and younger.

Taylor Swift, as one of country music's hottest stars, has moved the genre in new directions. She has younger fans, more urban and international audiences, and more pop sounds. Plus, she is more tech savvy and more marketing savvy. Pop country has become a new subgenre of traditional country music, one Taylor has helped create.

Country music singer Jason Aldean has credited Taylor Swift with introducing country to a new generation of fans. "Taylor has gone out and brought a whole new fan base to our world," Aldean said during an interview with *USA Today*. He also praised Swift as a trailblazer for writing and performing country music to which teenage girls can relate: "All these teenage girls that might not have listened to country before, she has brought them all into our genre. Nobody else is really doing that."

The Only Constant is Change

Taylor Swift and social media rose to popularity at the same time. The **evolution** of country music has also coincided with her career. As an Internet-age, music-driven pioneer, Taylor continues to attain crossover success by "not courting a traditional sound."

Along with her style, Taylor Swift's music and approach to promoting it have evolved with her career.

Her look has changed somewhat too over the years, but that's to be expected. She was a young woman of nineteen when her first album was released. Although her clothing and hairstyles tend to change with her music, her determination to record her own style of music has been constant. In her song "Change," Taylor sings about her hopes and aspirations in regard to succeeding, although she had been signed to the smallest record label in Nashville. Lyrically, it speaks of overcoming obstacles and achieving victory while staying true to herself.

Nothing stays the same. If an artist doesn't try new things, she might get left behind. New artists, songs, movies, and **products** are released every day. Taylor Swift has already established herself as someone who can adapt to change while maintaining her musical vision. She is a businessperson who knows how to make the most out of opportunities. She gets people to pay attention to and support her brand. What is the story behind her success? Read on to find out.

Taylor successfully brands her concerts.
On the Red tour, even her microphone was red.

This yearbook picture shows Taylor in school.

Chapter One

A Host of Ambition

Taylor Alison Swift was born December 13, 1989 in Reading, Pennsylvania. Named for American singer-songwriter and guitarist James Taylor, her mother, Andrea, believed that if Taylor had a gender-neutral name it would help her forge a business career: "If you got a business card that said 'Taylor' you wouldn't know if it was a guy or a girl."

Both Andrea and Taylor's father, Scott Swift, have careers in finance. Andrea, who often accompanies Taylor on tour, is practical; Scott, a stockbroker, is a dreamer. Andrea encourages Taylor to express herself; Scott offers financial advice with a dose of humor. This blend helped Taylor grow to be a creative yet practical person.

Taylor Swift's childhood home in Pennsylvania was on a Christmas tree farm.

A Performer from the Start

From the beginning, Taylor was an ambitious young girl. At age nine, she turned her attention to musical theatre and performed in Berks Youth Theatre Academy productions. She later traveled regularly to New York City for vocal and acting lessons. At age twelve, a computer repairman showed her how to play three chords on a guitar. This inspired her to write her first song, "Lucky You."

For Taylor, becoming one of the world's most influential singer-songwriters was natural. Having discovered poetry while in elementary school, she always loved words and knew they were fun and powerful. "Poetry is what turned me into a songwriter," she told *Rolling Stone*.

At six, Taylor became fascinated by LeAnn Rimes's voice. All she wanted to hear from then on was country, she said. "I loved the amazing female country artists of the nineties—Faith, [Hill] Shania [Twain], the Dixie Chicks—each with an incredible sound and standing for incredible things."

Then Taylor discovered **karaoke**. After finding a local contest, Taylor sang "every single week for a year and a half until I won." Her prize: opening for country and Southern rock singer Charlie Daniels. She was eleven.

Taylor also took advantage of the larger crowds at sporting events by singing the national anthem. Still, she knew that Nashville was country music's home. Eleven years old and ready to take the plunge, Taylor talked her mother into going to Nashville for vacation, with a stack of CDs she'd burned of herself singing karaoke.

Arriving on Nashville's Music Row, Taylor walked from recording studio to recording studio, giving every artists and repertoire division a CD, and announcing that she wanted a record deal. None came, but Taylor was not discouraged. "I realized I needed to be different," she said of the experience. "They saw that sort of thing every single day." Taylor then purchased a twelve-string guitar, and began writing songs about her feelings and middle school emotions.

Taylor's hard work began paying off when the Radio Corporation of America (RCA) offered her a "development deal," or "in-between record deal," that tracked her professional progress for one year. However, when the contract expired, she didn't re-sign. "They wanted to … keep me in development till I was probably eighteen. So I walked away from the biggest record company in Nashville," Taylor told NBC. Choosing to leave RCA was a bold move. Although it seemed to go against her careful planning, she followed her instincts and made a decision that proved to open other doors. At fourteen, Sony/ATV hired her as a songwriter.

On to Country Music's Capital

When Taylor was fourteen, her family relocated to Nashville, a move that allowed Taylor to pursue her career. She enrolled in Hendersonville High School, where she spent her days attending classes and writing songs for Sony/ATV. Taylor created lots of material because she didn't want to be underestimated or seem unprepared because of her young age.

Meanwhile, she still performed live. Universal Records' Scott Borschetta saw Taylor perform at the Bluebird Café and asked if she'd sign a record deal with him. Taylor was thrilled. Then she discovered Borschetta was actually leaving Universal to start his own record company, Big Machine. She took a deep breath and signed the contract. "I went with my gut instinct, which just said, 'Say yes.'" Success was not far away.

Endorsement Opportunities

As soon as Taylor's first album was released, companies began to approach her, offering endorsement opportunities. Over the years, these endorsement offers have become very **lucrative**. Among the multimillion-dollar companies whose products Taylor has endorsed are Diet Coke and Keds. Taylor has also expanded her opportunities by venturing into the perfume market. Her first scent, Wonderstruck, hit stores in 2011. Soon, two more successful fragrances, Wonderstruck Enchanted and Taylor, followed.

Taking Chances for Success

While Taylor's friends were spending hours at the mall, watching movies, playing video games, or going to parties, Taylor was writing songs. As a teen, she focused so much on building her career that some may feel she "missed out" on being a kid. Yet Taylor chose to take

Andrea, Scott, Taylor's brother Austin, and young Taylor pose for a family photo.

that chance. She knew what she wanted to do: become a musician and entrepreneur. She was driven by her passion, and went after it. Taylor won at her game of "chance."

Taylor's success proves that taking chances does not have to mean failure. Avoiding them, however, does mean missing out on what could be a one-time opportunity. If you are passionate about entrepreneurship, go for it. Put a plan in place. If it does not seem to be working out, learn from your mistakes, update your plan, and keep trying. That's how you carve out your path to successful entrepreneurship.

A replica of Taylor's tour bus is in the Country Music Hall of Fame and Museum.

Surprising Words on Success

Taylor admitted during an interview with *allBusiness* that since she was a little girl, she never "expected" success: "I think the biggest mistake you can make in life is to expect that you're entitled to success without working for it."

For young people who want success in the music industry, Taylor offers advice on working for success: "I would say that originality is the most important thing. Everyone has heroes. Don't try to be them. The most jaded people in the music industry are the ones who are incredibly talented, but haven't made it because what they do has been done over and over again."

Taking time to meet her fans is a big part of what Taylor does.

Chapter Two

Taylor Swift: The Brand

Taylor's brand identity began when she handed out the first recordings of her songs to studios on Nashville's Music Row, and later promoted herself through her MySpace page. From the very beginning, she has used her personality as much as her music to define her brand.

Since she is so visible, and because music is such a big business, people **speculate** that much of Taylor's brand is created to sell music, and are curious about how much of it is genuinely "Taylor." She has always been her own person, and uses her sense of humor and style to create an image that her fans can relate to. Although she is constantly connected to her music, she has successfully branched out into other business venues, including designing a line of shoes and perfumes. This has helped her become a household name, even among those who don't listen to country music.

Music and Fans

Most artists perform songs written by other people. Taylor Swift, however, is unique because she writes her own lyrics. This has led to her winning awards such as BMI Country Music Award's Songwriter of the Year, Grammy Artist of the Year, and the Young Hollywood Awards' Superstar of Tomorrow.

Taylor's singing career began in country. Her twelve-string guitar and sundress-and-cowboy-boot style of dress at the time reinforced her music's brand of storytelling lyrics. As her music evolved, it included more elements of pop, such as the double-stop, which is a music term that refers to two notes being played at the same time on a stringed instrument, such as a guitar. To keep pace with the evolution of her music, Taylor's appearance—and brand—have become more polished and cosmopolitan.

Taylor is consistently proving that she is not to be held within any specific genre of music. This move has landed her crossover success to mainstream radio that few artists have achieved. "I don't look at it as crossover as much as spillover," Taylor says.

Planning the Music

Taylor Swift has always been careful about how her music is introduced to the public and sold. For instance, her fourth album, *Red*, wasn't available for download until fans had plenty of time to pick up her CD in its entirety. She doesn't allow her music to be played on Spotify, since artists don't earn much money there.

Her concerts are carefully branded, too. During her Red tour, her microphone, guitars, and sets were red. Finally, the products she endorses at any given time are tied in to her current album. For example, when *Red* was released, a line of Taylor Swift merchandise at drugstores incorporated artwork from the album.

She Does It with Purpose

Taylor is just as deliberate with her appearance as she is with her music, marketing, and behavior choices. "The reality is what you wear matters. If you're a singer and on TV and in the living room of some twelve-year-old girl, she's watching what you're wearing and saying and doing ... I take [that responsibility] very seriously."

Remaining true to her reputation has been a challenge. "It would be really easy to say ... 'I do what I want, you raise your kids'," she admits. "But that's not the truth of it. Every singer out there is raising the next generation, so make your words count." Through all the media flurries, the difficulties growing up in the spotlight, Taylor has managed her image carefully and tastefully, which sets her apart from other music celebrities her age.

What Taylor does not do is just as much a part of her brand as what she does do. She does not smoke, and did not drink alcohol until age twenty-one. She dresses in a way that does not distract from her music.

Being hardworking is another aspect of her brand. She admits to making mistakes and works to correct them. An out-of-tune Grammy performance with singer Stevie Nicks is an example of something Taylor had to work to fix. She admitted her professional error and took voice lessons so she would be better during her next live performance.

Miley Cyrus, who played Hannah Montana, and Taylor perform at the Grammy Awards in 2009.

Philanthropy and Making a Difference

Taylor's entrepreneurial savvy has extended to **philanthropy**. In 2012, she helped raise money for homeless kids, donated $4 million to fund the Taylor Swift Education Center at Nashville's Country Music Hall of Fame, and made a public service announcement taking a stand against hate and the bullying of LGBT teens.

She has created music for helping other people, too. After reading about three-year-old Ronan Thompson's fight with cancer on his mother Maya Thompson's blog, *Rockstar Ronan*, Taylor penned the heart-wrenching song "Ronan" about his too-short life.

She performed it live only once—during the September 2012 Stand Up to Cancer telethon. Taylor then made the song available for download, and all the money it earned went to cancer-related charities.

Managing Life

Even with a management team, Taylor has the last say on major decisions. "When I'm in management meetings when we're deciding my future, those decisions are left up to me," she told *Bazaar*. "I'm the one who has got to go out and fulfill these obligations, so I should be able to choose which one I do or not. That's the part of my life where I feel most in control."

Taylor Swift has proved time and time again that she has what it takes to stay in the spotlight. She is careful with the image she presents publicly. This image has led to numerous endorsement deals, a new shoe line, cosmetics, three perfumes, and movie and TV appearances.

Swift Symbols

Some of Taylor's favorite things are parts of her brand, such as the number thirteen. She marks the number on her hand before concerts, talks about it on Twitter, and uploads Instagram shots of the number when she sees it. Wonderstruck Enchanted, one of her perfumes, is packaged in a box

Heart hands are just one of Taylor's signatures.

embossed with the number thirteen. Her fans mark "13" on their arms during concerts.

Another trademark "Taylor move" is that she makes a heart shape with her hands. The shape, Taylor says, means "something between 'I love you' and 'thank you.' It's just a sweet, simple message that you can deliver without saying a word." Those symbols bring Taylor to the minds of fans whenever they see them. That's smart branding.

Taylor endorses differen products, like Keds.

Chapter Three

Products of Success

Personal Style and Keds

Taylor has a style of her own, one that is adored by wearers of her line of Keds sneakers. The inspiration for this line, Taylor says, "goes back to my vintage springtime–summertime look … Keds are perfect with all of those looks."

The Keds campaign is targeted to "brave" girls between the ages of thirteen and twenty-four. It builds on a relationship between Taylor and Keds that started in 2012, when Keds sold red sneakers inspired by her album *Red*.

Scent-sational Swift

When creating her fragrance line Wonderstruck, Taylor wanted it to be "really romantic and magical." She wanted its wearers to "daydream about love and what it could be." Each bottle is decorated with charms. During

Wonderstruck is decorated with charms and named after some of Taylor's lyrics.

the charms' design process, Taylor asked fragrance designers to come to her apartment. "I wanted them to see that I had lots of star lanterns and bird cages. I wanted them to be inspired by all the things that are representative of what I love."

The fragrance took its name from Swift's song "Enchanted," which reflects on the first impression one person has of another: "I'm wonderstruck blushing all the way home." Taylor signed the deal with Elizabeth Arden to put out the signature scent in the fall of 2011. The spin-off fragrances Wonderstruck Enchanted and Taylor have since been released.

A Raw Deal

Not everything Taylor touches turns to gold, however. In January 2013, Taylor signed off on an endorsement deal with her favorite soda, Diet Coke, making her a brand ambassador for the calorie-free drink. Diet Coke's "You're On" ad campaign deal followed Taylor's lucrative contracts with CoverGirl, Sony Electronics, and Keds.

To promote the product, Coca-Cola launched a limited-edition Diet Coke can featuring Taylor's signature and a handwritten quote: "If you're lucky enough to be different, don't ever change." However, this was not enough for the campaign to avoid damaging criticism. The "You're On" campaign ended abruptly only a few months after its launch. Bloggers and others mocked the slogan on social media, forcing Coca-Cola to pull the ads.

A Classic Beauty

At twenty, Taylor's success and classic look of red lips and cat eyeliner turned heads. CoverGirl approached her to be a spokesperson, and a line of luxury cosmetics with her signature was launched. A longtime fan of CoverGirl, Taylor described the group as "great artists and actresses who are confident and still themselves. It was like a dream come true to be a part of the future of CoverGirl."

Live from New York!

In early January 2009, Taylor was invited to be a musical guest on NBC's *Saturday Night Live* (SNL). The show was taped on her mother's birthday. About the experience, she said, "I don't think either of us would've believed you [if you] told us a few years ago that we'd get to spend her birthday in New York City at *Saturday Night Live*. It's pretty unreal."

The appearance proved another "record" for Taylor. She was the youngest musical guest ever on SNL, and one of only a handful of country artists (among them were Garth Brooks, Dolly Parton, and Tim McGraw) to perform on the show in thirty-two years.

Then Came Hollywood

That same year, Taylor took on a short dramatic role in the CBS series *CSI: Crime Scene Investigation*. Filmed in California, the experience was a first for Taylor. She played

Taylor plays character Haley Jones in an episode of *CSI*.

the daughter of a motel manager who gets into serious trouble and is murdered, thus becoming the corpse of the crime scene investigation. A remix of one of her songs, "You're Not Sorry," was used as background music. The episode was a success—viewer numbers rose to 21 million, up by 3 million over the previous week.

At eighteen, Taylor made a cameo appearance in *Hannah Montana: The Movie*.

"I play[ed] one of my own songs and [was] just in the background of one of the scenes," she said of the experience. Taylor said that she had been "really excited" about the opportunity because "it's really cool when some of my little fans will come up with a Hannah Montana shirt on … I want to be like, 'Guess what? I got to be in that movie with her!'"

In the film *Valentine's Day* (2010), couples and singles in Los Angeles break up and make up because of the pressures and expectations of Valentine's Day. Taylor was tapped to play the role of Felicia, one that was fun, but unexpected: "For me to step outside of my comfort zone and try comedy … it was really wonderful."

Real-Life Hunger Games

Taylor hasn't just acted in films, she's written songs for them, too. She became famous for her diary-entry songs about ex-boyfriends and bullies, but her songs "Safe & Sound" and "Eyes Open" for the film *The Hunger Games* were a new experience. She describes getting into the lead character Katniss Everdeen's head as "a wonderful break. It's pretty intense writing about my own life, my own struggles. It was almost like a vacation to get to write from someone else's perspective."

What About Country Music?

About country music, Taylor says, "I think that there are so many kinds of country artist. People sing about their lives ... you write songs about what you know and the way you live your life—what you're proud of."

Every artist in country music, Taylor says, was raised a different way. "Some sing about pick-up trucks, some sing about bars and whiskey, and I sing about love and breakups. Whatever your priorities are, whatever your life is at the moment, that's what you sing about."

When it comes to writing her own songs, Taylor admits, "No one in my life has a safety pass. Anybody can be factored into a verse or chorus at some point. If you are going to know me, it's kind of like a given that you're probably going to be written about at some point."

Taylor not only wins awards but performs at lots of awards shows, like the MTV Awards in 2014.

Chapter Four

What the Future Holds

Now on the music scene for more than a decade, Taylor sometimes worries about her future. "I fret about the future … what my next move should be. What the move after that should be. How I am going to sustain this. How do I evolve?"

To stay on track, Taylor recognizes that she has to stay balanced. She now tries to bring more creativity to each album, but doesn't become so wrapped up in being different that she abandons her brand. "I have to try new things without becoming a new thing," she says. She tries to bring a freshness to her new work, and this is best demonstrated in her album, *1989*, which is almost entirely pop, a new angle of music for Taylor to explore.

The songs on *1989* follow her familiar themes of love and life. "As I've grown up, the things I've written about have completely evolved with how I was growing ... I'm still writing songs about my life ... It reminds me that the human experience isn't so lonely—it doesn't have to be so lonely."

About acting, Taylor says, "That's always something that's in the back of my mind, if the right thing came along ... It would have to be something so amazing that it would take me away from writing songs and touring, which would have to be an incredible script."

Taylor discovered "amazing" while reading the script for the character Rosemary in *The Giver* (2014). "I read scripts all the time, and I have only been in very tiny parts in one or two movies because I was always waiting for the right thing to come along to fully commit," Taylor explained. "When I read *The Giver*—first of all, I remembered reading the book, and I remember it deeply affected me in school," Taylor told *Teen Daily*. "But picturing the characters played by Jeff Bridges and Meryl Streep, and these incredible actors who had already signed on to the project, it was absolutely an honor to be approached to play Rosemary."

While acting remains one of Taylor's passions, and one she continues to explore, she is committed to songwriting, the music scene, and her fans.

Music's Next Steps

Both CD and digital sales have continuously decreased over the years. At the same time, more people are **streaming** music. On some websites, music can be streamed at no cost in exchange for listening to or watching ads. On others, if you pay a subscription fee, you can avoid the ads altogether.

Some people, including artists, think album sales are down because people are streaming music instead of purchasing it. Rather than sacrifice her music to free streaming services, Taylor makes an effort to control how much of her music is allowed to stream. For instance, with her fourth album, *Red*, she refused to allow it on streaming services such as Spotify, Xbox Music, and Rhapsody, hoping that it would mean more album sales. Her tireless campaign to promote the album seemed to pay off. *Red* sold over 260,000 records the first day.

In a *Wall Street Journal* op-ed piece, Taylor wrote that the success of recorded music, in

Taylor Swift performs with country stars Vince Gill, Emmylou Harris, and Kris Kristofferson in 2010.

her opinion, comes down to finding the proper price point for music and for keeping music fans interested by surprising them. "In recent years, you've probably read the articles about major recording artists who have decided to practically give their music away for this promotion or that exclusive deal. My hope for the future, not just in the music industry but in every young girl I meet ... is that they all realize their worth and ask for it."

Regarding album sales, Taylor says that people "are still buying albums, but now they're buying just a few of them. They are buying only the ones that hit them like an arrow through the heart or have made them feel strong or allowed them to feel like they really aren't alone in feeling so alone. It isn't as easy today as it was twenty years ago to have a multiplatinumselling album, and as artists, that should challenge and motivate us."

Being Different, Being Successful

Growing up in Pennsylvania and wanting to pursue country music for Taylor were "two different things." To make matters worse, she did not have many friends in school. "Kids would just heckle me. They would say, 'Go sing that country [music].' At that point, it dawned on me that I had to love being different or else I was just going to end up being dark and angry." People, she says, have not always been there for her, "but music always has."

By embracing her differences, Taylor Swift has not only created great music, but also a brand whose popularity goes far beyond the music industry. She has used her talent for business as successfully as her gift for songwriting, and has become one of today's leading celebrity entrepreneurs. In spite of rocky beginnings, today Taylor is a phenomenon. To others who feel alone or out of place she shares this advice: "If you're lucky enough to be different, never change."

Career Highlights Timeline

1989   Taylor Alison Swift born

2004   Hired as songwriter for Sony/ATV; family moves to Nashville

2005   Signs first record deal

2006   Releases first album, *Taylor Swift*

2008   Releases second album, *Fearless*

2009   Stars in a TV episode of *CSI*; plays a singer in *Hannah Montana: The Movie*

2010   Becomes youngest winner for Album of the Year Grammy (for *Fearless*); stars in *Valentine's Day*; releases third album, *Speak Now*; and announces endorsement deal with CoverGirl

2011   Releases her first perfume; named Billboard's Woman of the Year

2012   Releases her second perfume, and fourth album

2013   Becomes Diet Coke's "brand ambassador" and becomes first solo female artist to do a stadium concert tour in Australia since 1993

2014   Acts in the highly anticipated movie *The Giver*

Glossary

brand A famous person's public image. Include but not limited to what s/he does for a living, what s/he looks and dresses like, and how s/he acts.

celebrity Someone who is famous, although not necessarily for a particular talent.

endorsements Verbal or written seals of approval between companies and (usually) celebrities. In business terms, companies pay celebrities to use (or say they use) their products.

entrepreneur A businessperson. Often means someone who is clever at creating opportunities or making money.

evolution To change, usually over a period of time. As you change, you evolve.

genre A category of art (including music, movies, and literature). Different genres might be used as demographics.

karaoke Using a microphone to sing with music while the lyrics are displayed on a screen.

lucrative Having great financial value. An endorsement deal can be lucrative, for example.

philanthropy Helping a cause (typically humans, animals, or the environment) usually by donating money.

products Something you buy or sell. Entertainers are sometimes referred to as products.

speculate Using experience or history to guess what might happen in the future.

streaming Listening to music or watching video in real time instead of downloading a file to your computer and watching or listening to it later.

Further Information

Books

Johnson, Arne, and Karen Macklin. *Indie Girl: From Starting a Band to Launching a Fashion Company, Nine Ways to Turn Your Creative Talent into Reality*. San Francisco, CA: Zest Books, 2008.

Rankin, Kenrya. *Start It Up: The Complete Teen Business Guide to Turning Your Passions Into Pay*. San Francisco, CA: Zest Books, 2011.

Vaughan, Andrew. *Taylor Swift*. New York, NY: Sterling Publishing, 2012.

Websites

Network for Teaching Entrepreneurship
www.nfte.com
The Network for Teaching Entrepreneurship provides programs that inspire youth from low-income communities to recognize business

opportunities and to plan for successful futures. Search for programs in your area. Think you have what it takes to become and entrepreneur? Read "13 Telltale Signs You Might Be an Entrepreneur."

Taylor Talk
taylortalk.org
Join other "Swifties" on this free podcast as expert teams of hosts take you through the latest Taylor Swift news, song analyses, tour discussions, and more.

Videos

Justin Guitar.com
www.justinguitar.com
Explore the basic techniques you need to learn if you want to start playing slide guitar through a series of video lessons with London-based guitarist Justin Sandercoe.

Taylor Swift Official Website
taylorswift.com/media/videos/15853
Taylor's official website has home movies, videos for her perfumes, and personal v-logs. Chat with "Swifties" on Taylor's forum.

Index

Page numbers in **boldface** are illustrations.

About the Author

Tonya Maddox Cupp is a freelance writer and editor who shares Taylor Swift's affinity for words through reading and wordplay, as well as her appreciation for folk singers such as Patty Griffin and Lyle Lovett. Having come of age in the eighties, Cupp's first "pop" love was Madonna.

Cupp's passion for language led her to major in English at Westminster College in Fulton, Missouri. She has since developed a love for literary, feminist, and historical criticism. She currently lives near Indianapolis, Indiana.